HAL•LEONARD
INSTRUMENTAL
PLAY-ALONG

AUDIO
ACCESS
INCLUDED

**PLAYBACK+**
Speed • Pitch • Balance • Loop

# TENOR SAX

T0082042

| 2 | All I Do Is Win |
|----|----|
| 3 | Centerfold |
| 4 | Crazy Train |
| 6 | Don't Stop Believin' |
| 5 | Eye of the Tiger |
| 8 | Feel It Still |
| 10 | Havana |
| 12 | Kernkraft 400 |
| 13 | Land of a Thousand Dances |
| 12 | Sandstorm |
| 14 | Seven Nation Army |
| 15 | Sweet Caroline |
| 16 | We Are the Champions |

Audio arrangements by Peter Deneff

To access audio, visit:
**www.halleonard.com/mylibrary**
Enter Code
5905-1406-5633-5444

ISBN 978-1-5400-7202-3

Visit Hal Leonard Online at
**www.halleonard.com**

Contact us:
**Hal Leonard**
7777 West Bluemound Road
Milwaukee, WI 53213
Email: info@halleonard.com

In Europe, contact:
**Hal Leonard Europe Limited**
42 Wigmore Street
Marylebone, London, W1U 2RN
Email: info@halleonardeurope.com

In Australia, contact:
**Hal Leonard Australia Pty. Ltd.**
4 Lentara Court
Cheltenham, Victoria, 3192 Australia
Email: info@halleonard.com.au

# ALL I DO IS WIN

TENOR SAX

Words and Music by KHALED M. KHALED,
T-PAIN, CALVIN BROADUS,
CHRISTOPHER BRIDGES, WILLIAM ROBERTS,
JOHNNY MOLLINGS and LEONARDO MOLLINGS

# CENTERFOLD

TENOR SAX

Words and Music by<br>SETH JUSTMAN

# CRAZY TRAIN

TENOR SAX

Words and Music by OZZY OSBOURNE,
RANDY RHOADS and BOB DAISLEY

# EYE OF THE TIGER

TENOR SAX

Words and Music by FRANK SULLIVAN
and JIM PETERIK

# DON'T STOP BELIEVIN'

TENOR SAX

Words and Music by STEVE PERRY,
NEAL SCHON and JONATHAN CAIN

# FEEL IT STILL

TENOR SAX

Words and Music by JOHN GOURLEY,
ZACH CAROTHERS, JASON SECHRIST,
ERIC HOWK, KYLE O'QUIN,
BRIAN HOLLAND, FREDDIE GORMAN,
GEORGIA DOBBINS, ROBERT BATEMAN,
WILLIAM GARRETT, JOHN HILL
and ASA TACCONE

# HAVANA

**TENOR SAX**

Words and Music by CAMILA CABELLO, LOUIS BELL,
PHARRELL WILLIAMS, ADAM FEENEY, ALI TAMPOSI,
JEFFERY LAMAR WILLIAMS, BRIAN LEE, ANDREW WOTMAN,
BRITTANY HAZZARD and KAAN GUNESBERK

# KERNKRAFT 400

TENOR SAX

By EMANUEL GUENTHER
and FLORIAN SENFTER

**Moderate Techno**

# SANDSTORM

Words and Music by VILLE VIRTANEN
and JAAKKO SAKARI SALOVAARA

**Moderate Techno**

# LAND OF A THOUSAND DANCES

TENOR SAX

Words and Music by
CHRIS KENNER

# SEVEN NATION ARMY

TENOR SAX

Words and Music by
JACK WHITE

# SWEET CAROLINE

TENOR SAX

Words and Music by
NEIL DIAMOND

# WE ARE THE CHAMPIONS

Words and Music by
FREDDIE MERCURY

TENOR SAX